Little Books on Faith & Money

Also in the series:

Financial Anxiety by Brendan J. Barnicle
A Native Way of Giving by Forrest S. Cuch and Michael Carney

DONALD V. ROMANIK

Money
Legacies

CHURCH
PUBLISHING
INCORPORATED

little books
on faith &
money

Church Publishing
19 East 34th Street
New York, NY 10016
www.churchpublishing.org

Cover design by Jennifer Kopec, 2Pug Design
Typeset by Denise Hoff

Library of Congress Cataloging-in-Publication Data

Names: Romanik, Donald V., author.
Title: Money legacies / Donald V. Romanik.
Description: New York, NY : Church Publishing, [2021] | Series: Little books on faith and money | Includes bibliographical references.
Identifiers: LCCN 2021039211 (print) | LCCN 2021039212 (ebook) ISBN 9781640654570 (paperback) | ISBN 9781640654587 (ebook)
Subjects: LCSH: Wealth--Religious aspects--Christianity. | Money--Religious aspects--Christianity. | Finance, Personal--Religious aspects--Christianity.
Classification: LCC BR115.W4 R65 2021 (print) | LCC BR115.W4 (ebook) | DDC 241/.68--dc23
LC record available at https://lccn.loc.gov/2021039211
LC ebook record available at https://lccn.loc.gov/2021039212

Contents

Introduction

We all love stories. Storytelling is imbedded in our DNA as human beings. From earliest times, long before the written word, the history, customs, traditions, and practices of individual tribes and local communities were passed down from generation to generation, not as a recitation of facts but as stories. Stories were also used to explain the unexplainable—those mysteries such as birth, death, nature, and the existence of a higher power or force, eventually described as God. Furthermore, the stories were repeated time and time again, remembered and even internalized, so that those who listened became those who told. This process continued through the early millennia of the human experience. After a while, the stories were represented in pictures, symbols, characters, and eventually in letters and words, moving from oral tradition to written history. But the stories continued, sometimes altered or modified along the way, but still maintaining their incredible relevance and utter importance even to this day.

People of faith, or those who follow or practice a particular religious tradition, are especially fond of stories. Jewish and Christian heritage and custom have been passed down to us through stories—about creation, sin, floods, slavery, freedom, laws, prophets, angels, and, ultimately, redemption and resurrection. The Gospels, including those that never made it into the Bible, are stories about the life and teachings of Jesus as told by his disciples to other followers and eventually written down.

While we love to tell stories, we also love to talk about ourselves, especially those qualities and experiences of which we are most proud. Even the most introverted person will lighten up and be willing to respond when asked about their job, their family, or their accomplishments. Parents love to talk about their children, and grandparents are never hesitant to brag about their grandchildren and even show pictures to total strangers. Telling our story is an essential element of the human experience and is the precursor to making connections, establishing relationships, and falling in love.

Our storytelling tradition extends into our faith communities and is an important part of our worship and fellowship activities. The Liturgy of the Word, the first part of our communal worship as Episcopalians, includes listening to the stories of the people of Israel, the life and teachings of Jesus, and the experiences of his early followers. Our favorite preachers are often those who make the Gospels come alive by sharing their own personal journeys and experiences. Churches with active newcomer ministries provide opportunities for visitors or seekers to tell their stories. This type of engagement is not only an effective evangelism tool but also a way for church leaders to learn more about the prospective member and how they might be incorporated into the life of the community. We find out about people's backgrounds, families, careers, health conditions, hobbies, and even culinary abilities and food preferences. There seem to be very few limits on the information we seek and share in our parish family settings. Or are there?

If a congregation is truly serious about welcoming a newcomer into the body of Christ rather than a liturgical social club, these conversations must morph beyond general information and begin to delve into a person's desire and longing for a relationship with God. As the relationship deepens, the general questions should become more specific and begin to focus on the individual's spiritual side, especially as they begin to participate in more formal Christian formation opportunities. Questions like:

"What was your religious tradition growing up?"

"What are you looking for in a church home?"

"How and why did you decide to become part of our community?"

Or posing the most direct and poignant prompt: "Tell us about your spiritual journey."

This often begins the important process of transforming a seeker into a newcomer, a newcomer into a member, and a member into a disciple. This is what a church should be all about. Through telling and listening to our stories, we deepen our connections to God, each other, and the wider community.

This is not easy stuff. Asking a stranger about their relationship with God, or sharing your own spiritual experiences, creates a seismic shift in the process of establishing or building a relationship in a church setting. It can be intimidating, embarrassing, and intimate at its core. But most of us acknowledge that at some point in our church communities, the conversations need to shift to core matters of faith and a relationship with God.

As difficult as these faith-related conversations may be, there is a related topic that may feel more challenging, intimidating, embarrassing, and even intimate. In the process of incorporating people into our church communities, what if we asked questions like these:

"What was your family's financial situation growing up?"

"How did your family express its values through its spending practices?"

"When did you first learn and appreciate the value of money?"

"Do you consider yourself a spender or a saver?"

Or, "Tell us your money story; tell us about your financial journey."

The response may be: "What? Stop! It's bad enough that you are asking me about my faith. My money story and my financial journey are none of the church's business."

It's true. Talking about money is still the big taboo, especially in church circles—and especially among Episcopalians. We talk about everything else in church—the most intimate details of our lives, including health and even our relationships. What is it about money that makes it so off-limits in faith-based conversations? Is it none of the church's business to ask their members to tell their money stories along with other essential aspects of their lives? If we ask questions about faith, why can't we ask about money? What would Jesus say?

It's pretty amazing how much Jesus talks about money. In the New Testament, Jesus offers more wisdom and has more to say about money than any other subject other than the "kingdom of God." Eleven of his forty or so parables were about money or use money to illustrate his message. We all know the story about the hidden treasure and the pearl, the parable of the talents where the master entrusts his servants with money, and the parable of the rich man and Lazarus in which roles are reversed in the afterlife. While these are familiar stories, I think we often fail to recognize that they deal directly and specifically with money.

In addition to his parables, some of Jesus's most profound encounters involved people's complicated relationships with money and riches. In Luke 19, we meet Zacchaeus, an unscrupulous tax collector who confesses his wrongdoings and makes amends by agreeing to give half his possessions to the poor and pay back those he cheated with four times the amount. Jesus's immediate response to this bold move by Zacchaeus are the words: "Today salvation has come to this house . . ." (Luke 19:9a).

On the other hand, we have Jesus's interaction with a young man who asks him what he must do to inherit eternal life. After the young man assures Jesus that he keeps all the commandments of the law, Jesus says the following: "You lack one thing; go, sell what you own, and give the money to the poor, and you will have treasure in heaven; then come, follow me" (Mark 10:21). Mark tells us that man walks away in sadness because he had great wealth.

While we may decide to sidestep the message of the parables, it is much more difficult to ignore these bold and clear interpersonal encounters. These challenging words from Jesus continue to shake us up to this very day, especially for those of us who have accumulated some financial resources. Is Jesus actually saying that our individual salvation is dependent on giving all our worldly possessions to the poor? Immediately after the rich young man leaves the scene, Jesus is even more direct: *"Again I tell you, it is easier for a camel to go through the eye of a needle than for someone who is rich to enter the kingdom of God"* (Matthew 19:24).

However we may interpret these challenging passages, Jesus is clearly instructing us that, as Christians, we need to confront our relationship with money. These two stories imply that Zacchaeus directly acknowledged his unhealthy and corrupt attitude toward money and decided to help others, while the rich young man allowed money to interfere with his relationship with God. Throughout the Gospels, Jesus uses money as a tool and metaphor for illustrating the limitations of human priorities and the need to shift to a healthier and more life-giving attitudes toward wealth. He drives home this point in the Sermon on the Mount when he tells us:

Do not store up for yourselves treasures on earth, where moth and rust consume and where thieves break in and steal; but store up for yourselves treasures in heaven, where neither moth nor rust consumes and where thieves do not break in and steal. For where your treasure is, there your heart will be also. (Matthew 6:19–21)

In preaching about the kingdom of God using the beloved Beatitudes as an illustration, Jesus was aware of the significant challenges we face in trying to follow his way. And, in this passage and others, Jesus was willing to name those impediments to embracing his message. This bold statement clearly suggests that while many things may interfere with or distract us from a true relationship with God, money is at the top of the list. And that is why money should be an important discussion topic in the church.

While many of us may have issues with Jesus's exhortation to the rich young man to sell all his belongings and give the proceeds to the poor, most of us would agree that money, and how we spend it, is the clear indication of our values and priorities. Our monthly credit/debit card statement reveals more about ourselves than any other record or document. Furthermore, money defines who we are to the outside world, and permeates our work, our friendships, our social standing, and our access to necessities like food, housing, and health care. In our society, money equates success, influence, and power. Even our closest friends judge us based on how much money we have and, more importantly, how we spend it. For example, "She doesn't have a lot of money, but she is an incredibly generous person," or "What does he do with all his money? He clearly doesn't spend it on himself."

Whether we like it or not, money also affects our self-worth—the way we look, act, and function in society. We feel better about ourselves when we have money in our pocket or in the bank and less self-confident if we are experiencing a level of financial hardship. Unfortunately, these societal and personal attitudes around money lead to unhealthy and sometimes tragic results: massive credit card debt, real estate foreclosures, bankruptcy, and even suicide.

Whether we have a little or a lot of money, our spending patterns not only define us as consumers, but also as followers of Jesus. Money is not only about our values and priorities; money lies at the heart of Christianity and the fundamental premise that God created everything and everything ultimately belongs to God. This precept is totally contrary to our consumer society, our sense of entitlement, and the economic theory that everything we earn belongs to us.

Fundamental to a Christian view of money is how we should give it away. As followers of Jesus, our only response to an all-generous God is to be generous in return. And while we can exercise our response in ways other than with money, financial generosity is key, especially in our economic system and consumer-driven society. That is what stewardship is about—caring for and managing all of God's resources, especially those for which we have a particular responsibility—our own money. Therefore, stewardship is not only one aspect of Christian life, it is the summation and culmination of how we live as followers of Jesus. Jesus talks so much about money because it is a tangible way we participate in building up God's kingdom here on earth in our own time and place.

Before we can embrace and practice Christian stewardship to our fullest, each of us needs to discern and acknowledge those obstacles that prevent us from doing so. These obstacles are not necessarily evil or even negative; rather, they represent our day-to-day attitudes and experiences around money that have developed over our lifetime. Talk leads to action. Therefore, we need to talk about money with our partners, our families, and the wider community as part of the work of change and transformation.

Stewardship lies at the heart of who we are and what we do as Christians. Since the way we handle money is an important component of stewarding God's creation, the church must talk about money, and, more importantly, encourage and empower its members to do the same. Rather than it being none of the church's business, the personal money stories of its members provide insights into hopes, dreams, spiritual longings, need for community, and, most important, their relationships with God.

This is not easy stuff. Since secular culture proclaims that money defines us, it not surprising that many of us feel ashamed of our relationship with money at times and find it difficult to discuss. Church leaders should be willing to address the financial aspects of spiritual well-being. It is not so much about what is in our bank accounts but about helping us examine our relationships with money. Our individual relationship with money also affects the wider community. When we explore the issue of money for ourselves, we can more effectively address the financial well-being of our congregations. People with unhealthy attitudes about money in their personal lives cannot effectively manage or address the financial affairs of their faith community.

Jerry Colonna is an executive coach who uses the skills he learned as a venture capitalist to help other entrepreneurs. He draws on his variety of experiences to help clients design a more conscious life and make changes to their career to improve performance and satisfaction. Previously, Colonna was a partner with JPMorgan Partners (JPMP), the private equity arm of JPMorgan Chase. He joined JPMP from Flatiron Partners, which he launched in 1996 with his partner, Fred Wilson. Flatiron became one of the most successful early-stage investment programs in New York City.

Colonna's book *Reboot: Leadership and the Art of Growing Up*, published in 2019, is a journey of radical self-inquiry, helping CEOs reset their lives by sorting through the emotional baggage holding them back professionally and, even more importantly, in their relationships. In *Reboot*, Colonna inspires leaders to hold themselves responsible for their choices and for the possibility of achieving their dreams.

In chapter 1 of the book, titled "Passing Go," Colonna talks about his growing up as one of seven children in a two-bedroom apartment on the ground floor of a small Brooklyn building owned by his grandfather. He tells his money story using the game Monopoly as his life's metaphor. He loved the game not only because he felt great about amassing money, but because he was able to surprise people with what he was capable of doing. For Colonna, money was safety and his pursuit of money was a way of escaping poverty, chaos, and the streets of his childhood. He describes his financial pursuits and how, for him, money and success meant admiration, acknowledgment, and accolades as ends unto themselves. Colonna also talks about how becoming rich would lead him to thoughts about suicide and how, through a process of radical self-inquiry, he found his way to his own truest self.

At the end of the chapter, Colonna suggests a series of questions to help his readers confront their own money stories and how their belief systems around money from earliest childhood shaped their chosen careers, their definitions of success and failure, their view of the value of other people's work, and even their own sense of worthiness. While Colonna addresses other critical areas around leadership and growth in his book, he begins with money—the most basic element in the hearts and minds of the leaders he is trying to inspire, change, and ultimately transform.

It appears that Jesus and Jerry Colonna are on the right track. Our attitudes about money do tell us a lot about who we are and how we function in our family, our church, and the world. Moreover, in a very real sense, our personal money story and our faith journey often overlap. Money permeates everything we do, including how we struggle to live as faithful Christians. In many situations it is often difficult to determine where the money legacy ends and where the spiritual journey begins. For this reason, it is high time to tell our own money stories in our local faith communities and encourage our siblings in Christ to do the same. Quite frankly, as followers of Jesus, pilgrims on the journey, and would-be disciples, we have no other choice. Yes, money is all of our business.

In addition to our personal lives, money is critical to our life as a congregation. It keeps the lights on, pays the clergy and other staff, and enables us to engage in our mission and ministry. Churches, like individuals, also participate in our consumer society and are judged, both within and outside ecclesial structures, on the basis of budgets and wealth. Therefore, we also need to talk about money and our relationship with it as a community of faith. How we spend our money as a congregation indicates our priorities and says more about who we are than any mission statement or strategic plan.

Each of us has a personal money story that developed early in life and stems from our family of origin. This legacy shapes our attitudes about money even as we age, including how we spend it, save it, and give it away. Consequently, our economic status as children often determines our approach to money during our entire lives even if our personal financial situation changes over time. This may be especially true for people who grow up with a feeling of scarcity or economic insecurity and later achieve a greater level of financial success. Similarly, economic privilege as a child often stays with us although our financial condition may diminish.

Like other individual attributes, people bring their money personalities to their adult relationships, their workplaces, and even their volunteer and avocational activities. In the church context, for example, each member of the vestry or other administrative council, finance, or property committee brings their money legacy to the table, which may affect how they approach a particular issue or concern and even how they make decisions. Given this reality, the collective money stories of individual members, especially leaders, can profoundly affect the larger parish enterprise.

Furthermore, individual parishes and congregations, especially those with a wealthy historical past, also have money legacies that shape their attitudes and spending habits even when their demographics and financial circumstances change. As with individuals, a congregation's financial management and budgeting practices are developed over time and reflect spending priorities that often span generations. For this reason, congregations also need to tell their money stories to examine possible unhealthy relationships or experiences with money in the past, and, more importantly, use money in effective and spiritually healthy ways for current and future ministry.

We cannot talk about money from either a personal or congregational point of view without acknowledging the significant impact of COVID-19. As we continue to navigate the new circumstance, we need to appreciate the economic impact of the pandemic on many of our churches and their members. While some segments of the population have been affected more than others, this experience has and will continue to be part of our money legacies, even for those of us who prospered during this dark period. Furthermore, we are only beginning to discern the long-term impact on church membership, attendance, and active participation. While health and safety concerns have been the priority, economic consequences are also critical both now and moving forward.

This book is intended to help faith communities encourage and facilitate a process for both individuals and the congregation as a whole to confront their money legacies, share their ongoing money stories, and develop more healthy and life-giving attitudes about the role of money in the Christian context. I will begin by telling my own money story growing up in a blue-collar family and living with an immigrant grandmother who had a profound influence on my attitude toward work, self-sufficiency, thrift, and generosity. Next will come the money stories, as I know them, of some of the parishes I have been affiliated with throughout the years and how their financial legacy has impacted their mission and ministry. Last, I will encourage you to do the same sort of storytelling and provide some suggestions on how to begin and sustain this process.

I realize that conversations about money are challenging, if not taboo, especially among people of faith. Consequently, as we embark on this journey together, let us do so thoughtfully and prayerfully, and without judgment or guilt. Our money legacies and ongoing money stories are essential keys to who we are as individual Christians and Christian communities. They help form and shape who we are and what we do. During this time of incredible uncertainty and change in the church and the world, these conversations may also be a way of grounding us and focusing us on the work of the gospel and how we respond to God's call in this time and place.

1 ▪ *Telling My Money Story*

I was born in 1954 and grew up in New Haven, Connecticut, during the golden age of the "American Dream." All four of my grandparents emigrated from Poland in the early 1900s and my early life centered around St. Stanislaus Roman Catholic Church and School. My father, a WWII Navy veteran, never finished high school but worked his way up through various union positions at Winchester Repeating Arms Company. Like many smaller cities in the Northeast, New Haven was the home of manufacturing facilities at that time and provided employment to thousands of unskilled laborers, including the sons and daughters of European immigrants as well as the growing African American community. Despite the growing dominance of Yale University in the economy and real estate of the city, New Haven at the time was overwhelmingly white, ethnic, and blue collar.

Along with my father, two of his brothers also worked at and retired from Winchester's, creating a sense of family loyalty and gratitude to the company that transcended any employment relationship. While my father identified himself as a "shop rat," he also knew that he was able to support his family through the sweat of his brow and an honest day's work. This traditional work ethic may be somewhat anachronistic today, but it permeated the culture of my immediate and extended family and still shapes my current attitudes and perceptions. While I appreciate the barriers to economic and social advancement in contemporary society, as the grandson of immigrants and the first generation in my family to attend college, I still believe that America is the land of opportunity.

My comprehension of money goes back to my earliest memories, with the dime being central to this awareness. To this day, when I see or touch a ten-cent piece, I think of the dime Mrs. McCoy, an elderly friend of my mother's, would put in my small hand while greeting me with a kiss, as she did with all the children of our neighborhood, or watching the coin bounce in the felt-lined collection basket passed by the ushers in church. Having much more value in the late 1950s than today, coins were ubiquitous and plentiful. They filled pockets and purses and jingled and rang like bells when poured onto our Formica and chrome kitchen table before being counted and swept up once again. At the tender age of six, I would be sent by my mother to Lev's Market around the corner with her change purse in hand. Mrs. Lev would remove the coins she required, and I would carry back the groceries and the change purse with a sense of pride and accomplishment. These early recollections suggest that as I became more involved in business and commerce, my attitude toward money morphed from amazement to amusement to responsibility.

During these more innocent times of a cash economy and long before credit cards or even personal checking accounts, my mother, as the person responsible for the family budget, would organize her business transactions with the help of budget envelopes. This brown cardboard portfolio, tied with a string, contained individual, attached envelopes with distinct labels. My mother would cash my father's weekly paycheck and then carefully and thoughtfully insert the bills into their appropriate categories, the amount determined by the financial obligations of the week: Rent, Utilities, Groceries, Insurance, Car, Entertainment, and Other. While she usually performed this task outside of my presence, I would often come across this simple but effective accounting instrument when I would occasionally snoop through the top drawer of the mahogany chest-on-chest in my parent's bedroom. Like an abacus used to teach basic arithmetic, my mother's budget envelopes taught me, very early on, that money was finite and needed to be allocated to specific uses and purposes. Furthermore, "living within one's budget" became an early precept of my economic philosophy.

In 1962 my parents bought their first and only house for $15,000. I remember the excitement of the closing in an art deco–style office building in downtown New Haven with multiple people passing and signing documents culminating in hugs, handshakes, and big smiles. Home ownership was and still is the hallmark of living the "American Dream" and my parents clearly savored their new sense of financial independence. In addition to having my own room, a yard to play in, and cousins across the street, the new house also allowed for my maternal grandmother, "Babci," to move in with us and become part of our household. Babci provided built-in childcare, allowing my mother to go to work, and contributed additional funds for the household budget as she paid room and board. Most importantly, Babci was a significant presence, if not a force, with a profound influence on all aspects of my life, including my concept of money.

Katherine Paterak immigrated to the United States from Poland in 1912. She was sixteen years old and orphaned, with all her worldly goods in a steamer trunk, which is still one of my most cherished possessions. Lacking any financial resources, Katie was sponsored by a strong-willed, domineering aunt in New Haven, who paid for her passage and incidental expenses with the full expectation of being repaid for her efforts. Upon arriving in New York harbor and taking a train to New Haven, Katie had limited prospects for gainful employment. She even attempted to join the local convent but was unable to meet the financial dowry required for postulancy. She soon became employed as a domestic by a warm, loving Jewish family who taught her English, sent her to citizenship classes, and invested her salary wisely and prudently. Eventually, Katie paid back her aunt for the cost of her passage and then some.

Upon encouragement from her employers, Katie confronted her aunt one day as to why she continued to pay a financial obligation that had been fully satisfied. Her inquiry was met with an angry and cruel slap across the face, causing her to fall down a flight of stairs. Estranged from her only blood relation in the state, Katie continued to work and managed to save up $900 (about $10,000 today). In 1920, Katie married Stanley Gorecki, another Polish immigrant. Stanley had worked in an anthracite coal mine in eastern Pennsylvania, was drafted by the United States government, and was subjected to mustard gas in the trenches of France in WWI. Stanley returned to New Haven, worked sporadically in a foundry, and died of silicosis, a form of lung cancer, at the age of forty-two. As a young widow, Katie needed to support herself and her two daughters without the benefit of any public safety net.

Despite these hardships, Katie was always gainfully employed, supported her family, and was extremely generous to her family and wide circle of friends. Her hospitality was legendary; friends and strangers alike could come to her home at all hours of the day and night for good conversation, good food, and good drink. My mother recalls having the best of food, even during the dark days of the Depression, when many others went without.

Katie never looked back, never regretted her past, and never returned to her homeland. Her last contact with Poland was when she was informed in 1939 that her stepbrother had been shot to death when he refused to turn over his farm to the Nazi invaders. She was American through and through, and eternally grateful to her country for her social security check and small monthly widow's pension from the Veterans Administration. In addition to her room and board payments, Babci took us out to dinner on a regular basis and ensured that I always wore the appropriate clothing, especially good shoes and outwear. On Sunday afternoons she would often organize her dresser drawers, an outward symbol of her internal organization and mettle.

On a very regular basis my grandmother would give me the following advice: "Always remember, Donald, that God comes first but then the dollar." Initially, I thought that this adage was simply an unsophisticated, uneducated Polish immigrant grand-mother's way of explaining how she dealt with the challenges and hardships of life. Upon further reflection and experience, I realized that this seemingly simplistic advice was her profound way of describing her concept and experience of money, gen-erosity, and even stewardship. Babci left me $10,000 at her death in 1975, a modest sum by today's standards, but it almost paid my full tuition at Boston University School of Law. My grandmother reinforced in me the value of hard work, living within your means, saving for a rainy day, and what I like to call "thrifty generosity."

When Winchester's received a government contract to manu-facture the M-14 military service rifle, my father was able to work an additional fifteen hours a week of overtime for several years. Since overtime was paid at "time and one half," his usual paycheck was increased by almost 50 percent during this golden era in the economics of our family. We were able to take family vacations, buy consumer goods, and generally have some sense of financial security. When the M-14 contract came to an end and my father returned to working only forty hours a week, the family's economic situation changed abruptly, albeit fairly seamlessly. My sister and I were informed about the need for some belt tightening, but my mother's incredibly skillful budget discipline and Babci's continued generosity lessened the impact of this economic blow. While my sister and I assumed some modest student debt, my parents were able to send us both to the private colleges of our choice, an impressive accomplishment at that time and a virtually impossible challenge for most families under current economic circumstances.

During this period, St. Stanislaus Church, and other Roman Catholic churches for that matter, supported itself through the regular collection on Sunday mornings; "second collections" and special appeals; "stole fees" from weddings, funerals, and baptisms; contributions for memorial masses; and multiple events throughout the year, including the spring bazaar, the annual picnic, special dinners, and other occasional celebrations. Since everyone was obligated to attend Sunday mass under pain of sin, regular plate offerings, including those dollars dropped in the collection basket by my parents, provided a steady stream of income. My family also volunteered to work at the various fundraising events and I have fond memories of serving up fried dough with tomato sauce and kielbasa sandwiches on rye bread to hungry crowds. Fundraising for the school included the sale of candy, Christmas cards, wrapping paper, and weekly contributions to help build the new motherhouse for the good Sisters of Nazareth. My family's participation in nonreligious charitable giving was usually limited to door-to-door solicitations by neighbors for various health-related causes. It was not until becoming an adult, and actually an Episcopalian, that I first encountered the concept of stewardship and the practice of regular, disciplined giving, including pledges.

While I always earned a modest allowance, I regularly worked during my high school years, initially selling soda and hotdogs during football season at Yale Bowl and, when I turned sixteen, as a clerk at the neighborhood drug store, one of my favorite jobs of all time. Very early on I adopted the same budgetary discipline I learned from my mother and saved money for various school activities, including field trips and proms, as well as Christmas and birthday gifts for members of my family. My mother often agreed to go "half" on some major purchases, which not only resulted in cost savings but taught me the benefits of financial partnerships and the need for "skin in the game." During two summers of my college years, I worked at my father's beloved Winchester's during the overnight shift. That experience helped me appreciate my father's thirty-four years as a loyal employee and the inherent dignity and value of an honest day's work no matter how routine or repetitive. These early working years only reinforced those deeply imbedded values of thrift, budgets, savings, and economic independence.

Through Babci's financial legacy, my personal savings, and a monthly allowance of $250 from my parents, I was able to get through three years of law school at Boston University, driving back and forth to Hartford in my 1967 Ford Galaxie 500 to see my college girlfriend turned fiancée. In 1979, having virtually depleted my savings after purchasing an engagement ring, I graduated, started a new job, rented an apartment, and married Margaret on Michaelmas of that year.

When a couple marries and creates a new economic unit, they not only combine assets and liabilities, but more importantly they bring two separate and sometimes divergent money legacies to the relationship. Fortunately for Margaret and me, while the circumstances of our family backgrounds were vastly different, our economic values and attitudes toward money meshed perfectly. Thus, we created a new money story and forged a financial legacy that we passed on to our children.

Calling Margaret and me "thrifty" back in 1979, or even now, would be an understatement. We began our life together with a combined income of $20,000 and a negative net worth, but through budgetary discipline and living within our means, our economic situation gradually improved. While Margaret's return to graduate school necessitated some additional debt, new job opportunities for her and career advancement for me continued this positive trajectory. We bought our first house in 1983 and were extremely grateful to have assumed a mortgage rate of only 10.5 percent when market rates were as high as 14 percent. We had our first child in 1985, moved to a bigger house, had a second child, and continued to enhance our economic position over the years.

We also became affiliated with a local Episcopal church early in our marriage. Margaret was a cradle Episcopalian and I, having been exposed to the attractiveness of this tradition in college, was received as a young adult. It was there at Church of the Good Shepherd in Hartford that I first learned the theology and practice of stewardship. We pledged, I for the very first time, and also contributed significant time and talent to the various church ministries, including vestry, choir, and youth. I served as senior warden for several years and both of us continued our church involvement in subsequent parish settings.

Margaret and I never deprived our two sons of all the basic necessities and provided some luxuries as well—the so-called finer things in life. But we always taught and modeled those same values of working hard, saving money, and living within our means. Both boys graduated from college without any student loans and entered the work force with some level of financial security. Our younger son, James, was especially aware of money and its value at an early age. He was very curious about prices and often tried to peek at restaurant checks not only to determine the cost of the meal but to determine whether it was worth the price. During his first home visit in his freshman year at college, James inquired as to our financial capacity to fund his education and even asked about his health insurance options after he graduated. Margaret and I realize that our financial legacy to our children exceeds any amount of a gift or ultimate bequest. We are proud that both our sons, David, an Episcopal priest, and James, a fundraising professional, have developed healthy attitudes toward money, generosity, and stewardship.

My "money story" describes growing up in a family of modest means followed by a gradual but steady growth in income, savings, and financial security over a period of forty years. It reflects the cultural realities of the times in which I grew up, along with my race, gender, and ethnic background. It also shapes and even explains how I have and continue to function in both my household and the marketplace. Thriftiness and frugality are still the order of the day. It does not take much for me to revert to those leaner economic times and, even now, question spending money at the most modest levels.

This money legacy has also impacted my work life. When I first became president of the Episcopal Church Foundation (ECF) in 2005, I began to work with our chief operating officer, taking full advantage of his skill and expertise, to manage the budget prudently and cautiously, without negatively affecting the underlying mission of the organization. It is how we spend money rather than how much we spend that ultimately determines our effectiveness and impact.

My money legacy has also impacted my stewardship journey. While I fully believe that everything I have comes from a gracious and generous God, I also acknowledge the benefits of the values learned from my family of origin. I have been profoundly impacted by my grandmother's story of coming to this country with almost nothing, and through perseverance and hard work, managing to raise two daughters alone and achieving some level of financial independence and dignity. I honor my parents for achieving middle class status without the benefit of formal education or family wealth. I truly believe that my parents and grandparents earned and deserved everything they worked for. At the same time, I am fully aware of white privilege and the impact of systemic racism on the opportunities of millions of Americans, especially now, given the vast economic disparities in the US economy. After all, my immigrant grandparents were white Europeans and, for the most part, were welcomed to America, at least for their cheap labor. But their story is still part of my story. My challenge is to reconcile my own money story with the stories of those with a different financial reality or economic trajectory. The American Dream is not dead but clearly on life support. As we share our money stories and legacies, let us also recommit to making this ideal a reality once again.

2 ▪ *Churches Have Money Stories Too*

Prior to the proliferation of church websites and other digital advances, parishes in a clergy transition would publish a hard copy, printed profile that would be sent to prospective candidates interested in applying for the vacant rectorship. Some of these profiles were rather elaborate, with professional photographs and high-quality paper stock. After an introductory page from the search committee, the first section of this document was inevitably the parish history. Depending on the church or its geographic location, this section would often go on for multiple pages and would often include details like a description of how and why the church was founded, a list of all previous rectors, and of course, a photo of the proverbial Tiffany window, whether authentic or a credible reproduction. The section on finances would include the annual operating budget and direct or indirect references to endowments or other permanent funds. There might also be a description of the parish's stewardship efforts, including the number of pledging units and the amount of the average pledge. Prior to having any direct conversations with the parish leadership, a savvy candidate would have to deduce the overall financial health of the congregation based on information in the profile. In other words, rather than stating it directly, the parish profile was a backhanded attempt to tell its money story both to itself and the wider church.

While some parishes in transition still prepare profiles, they tend to be fully digital and much more focused on what the congregation is looking for in a new rector, that is, preacher, teacher, administrator, evangelist, fundraiser, and community organizer. Much of the other information is usually available on the parish website. Furthermore, since technological advances in the search process have coincided with overall church decline, search committees need to be much more transparent about their finances, especially if sound financial oversight is one of the skill sets they are looking for in their new priest. Nevertheless, even during a time when they are fully in the spotlight, parishes are still reluctant to tell their money story in an open, honest, and direct way. Moreover, much like in the old days, any broader conversation about money tends to be relegated to the annual stewardship campaign or vestry budget conversations once the rector is in place.

The history of any organization, including a church, directly influences its current financial stability and sustainability. The history of the Metropolitan Museum of Art, for example, is the story of how a group of Gilded Age philanthropists donated the money and art collections to create one the greatest museums in the world. The same is true of multiple other arts organizations whose very existence is dependent on the generosity of their patrons and participants. These organizations tend to be much more aware of this reality and are willing to talk about it openly and freely. They know that their money story is a compelling case statement for continued financial support. Churches in general and Episcopal churches in particular are much more reluctant to engage in this process in any meaningful way. We may talk about our historic buildings and even the cost of restoration and repair during a capital campaign, but we will not discuss where the money came from to construct the buildings in the first place.

We will discuss this in greater detail in a subsequent chapter, but for now let me highlight: knowing and telling the money legacy and ongoing money story of your congregation is critical to its current financial health and ongoing economic sustainability. The money legacy of a faith community explains its past, influences the present, and shapes the future. Like telling your own personal money story, telling the money story of a congregation is an opportunity to engage the church community in discerning God's call right now and articulating a vision for the future.

Over the past forty or so years, Margaret and I have been associated with five different congregations. Four of them have rich histories and architecturally significant buildings and one of them is a typical suburban church built in the 1960s. All five have been and continue to be places of spiritual nourishment for their members and significant outreach to the wider community. While all of these faith communities have a unique history and background, they also have a money story—a financial legacy that has shaped their mission and ministry over many years, and, more importantly, will impact their future vitality and sustainability.

Telling the money story of a congregation is a somewhat complex but dynamic process that involves the active participation of a wide cross section of the community. I will provide some suggestions on how this can be done in a subsequent chapter. At this point, however, I want to share my thoughts and reflections around the money legacies of the parishes I know the best. Please know that these are my opinions, which are based on my own knowledge and personal experience. I share them not as the definitive word on the financial legacy of these remarkable faith communities, but as illustrations on how and why telling these stories is so important.

Samuel Colt was an American inventor, industrialist, and businessman who established Colt's Patent Fire-Arms Manufacturing Company and made the mass production of revolvers commercially viable. Colt's manufacturing methods were sophisticated, and he was one of the first to use the assembly line efficiently. He died in 1862 as one of the richest men in America. The building for a Episcopal parish was commissioned by Elizabeth Jarvis Colt, the widow of Samuel Colt, and completed in 1867. The church and its associated parish house were designed by Edward Tuckerman Potter, and serve as a memorial to Samuel Colt and members of his family. Just up the hill from the church and overlooking his armory, Samuel Colt built Armsmear, a stately Italian-style villa accompanied by greenhouses, ponds, fountains, and a deer park. After Elizabeth Colt died in 1905, the house was converted to a home for Episcopal women under the terms of her will. The residential community to this day is administered by the Colt Trust of which the parish is also a beneficiary. Both Armsmear and the church campus were listed on the National Register of Historic Places in 1975 and became contributing properties to the Coltsville Historic District in 2008.

The money legacy and the ongoing money story of this congregation has always been very clear. But for the generosity of Elizabeth Colt, it would have never been established and would not exist today. When Margaret and I first began to attend the parish in 1981, it was made very clear to us who was still in charge—evidenced by Elizabeth's imposing and severe portrait in the parish house and the many memorial plaques throughout both historic buildings. Even the senior warden at the time indicated that her role was to make decisions based on what Mrs. Colt would want her to do.

The immediate neighborhood, just south of downtown, consisted primarily of low-income residents, including various subsidized housing projects and, during our time there, under the leadership of a dynamic rector, the parish was involved in significant, hands-on outreach and community involvement. The congregation was dominated by elderly residents of Armsmear and former neighbors who had moved to the suburbs, but a program of civic involvement began to attract younger professionals from the area and the place began to grow. While stewardship revenue increased during this period, the parish continued to rely on the beneficence of the Colt trustees.

When I served as senior warden, the rector and I would make our annual pilgrimage to the meeting of the trustees, presided over by a Dickensian chairman perched behind a large mahogany desk, and request our allowance to continue our "good work." Over time, as the membership changed, the trustee meetings became far less auspicious. Nevertheless, it was clear to us, the vestry, and the wider congregation that we were grateful wards and dependent on the largesse of Mrs. Colt's legacy for our very survival. Despite its very small congregation, thanks to the trust, the parish continues to enjoy significant resources for ongoing restoration and funding for a full-time rector. One can argue the economic disparities among urban congregations in the area was exacerbated by the existence of the Colt Trust. For purposes of this discussion, however, this particular money story has and continues to shape its mission, ministry, and very existence.

We left that congregation in 1996 and joined our son, who was singing in the men and boys' choir at a downtown church. The history of this congregation is directly tied to that of the Episcopal Church in the United States. The original property, purchased in 1762, was confiscated during the Revolutionary War and not recovered until 1784, the same year that Samuel Seabury, a native of Groton, Connecticut, was consecrated in Aberdeen, Scotland, as the first bishop in the American church. The original white clapboard meetinghouse, completed in 1795, was replaced by a gothic-style church designed by Ithiel Town and consecrated in 1829.

Over the years, the parish served as the spiritual home of many of the first families of the state, including those who founded banks, insurance companies, hospitals, museums, and many other institutions. The walls of the church are filled with memorial plaques honoring those with notable names like Morgan, Goodwin, and Sigourney. There were even some older parishioners who remembered the time when limousines and their chauffeurs would line Main Street on Christmas, Easter, and other major holidays. As a result of the philanthropy of these wealthy families, a substantial endowment accumulated which, during my time there, was one of the largest in the diocese.

Like many, if not most, of these resourced, urban congregations, the demographics of this church changed over the years, with all the limousines completely disappearing. Despite its solidly middle-class congregation, including a substantial West Indian population, there continued to be a sense of privilege and entitlement that was perpetuated, if not encouraged, by the senior leadership. Even as the membership began to dwindle, the budget continued to increase and was funded overwhelmingly by the endowment. Stewardship—and its place in a spiritual life—was an afterthought. Rather than conducting a capital campaign, the leadership decided to fund extensive building restorations through endowment funds, which only enhanced the prevailing attitude that money was no object.

During the years I served in leadership, I, too, bought into this sense of entitlement, although even in this position I was never privy to all the financial records. It was only after a clergy retirement and the hiring of an interim rector that I finally learned about the spending excesses of the recent past. By the time a permanent successor was elected, the congregation was on the path to fiscal responsibility and greater financial transparency that has continued to the present time.

This congregation never told its money story in any organized or focused way. The implicit message suggested there was enough money for anything and everything—reinforced by free catered lunches, subsidized bus trips to New York and Boston, and opulent floral displays for Christmas and Easter. Lack of financial transparency and an almost nonexistent focus on stewardship or individual giving only exacerbated this sense of unlimited largesse. Had the parish told its money story, the leadership may have engaged in more prudent fiscal management, and, even more importantly, the congregation may have been better nurtured and developed as stewards of all this bounty. The people of our first parish regularly told the money story of the church and knew and appreciated that its very existence depended on the Colt Trust. By not doing so, however, this second congregation created and perpetuated an unhealthy culture of entitlement that took years to dismantle and change.

After some unpleasant happenings, my wife and I moved our parish affiliation. Organized almost one hundred years prior, our new congregation experienced rapid growth in the 1930s and '40s and undertook a threefold building program, constructing a new church in 1962. The history of the parish is basically the history of the community, a desirable, first ring suburb of about sixty-five thousand people. Although it has become more diverse over the years, especially in certain designated neighborhoods, the area is 80 percent white with a high median household income. The parish is overwhelmingly white and a microcosm of the community. While there is a substantial and stable senior population, the church does attract young families, warranting the need for active youth programming.

This congregation tells its money story regularly and directly, especially during the annual fund campaign. The basic message is that "if you want it, you have to pay for it." And, if the campaign is running under budget, the message morphs into threatened cuts in popular programs unless members increase their pledge. There are regular unapologetic appeals throughout the year and during our time there the budget was always in balance. While some people may have preferred a more theological or spiritual approach to stewardship and giving, the consumer-based message, especially by the rector, seemed to resonate among the membership. The "pay to play" money story seems to work well at least for the present.

Longing for a more urban and diverse church experience, Margaret and I moved to a new parish in 2017. At its founding in 1859, the common practice of churches was to raise funds for their operation by the rental of pews. This parish was a pioneer in the area by deciding to be a "free" church with no pew rents, where any person "no matter what his or her wealth or poverty" might find spiritual nourishment. Their first building, a former Unitarian meeting house, was moved stone by stone to the present site. Between 1892 and 1898, with the support of a gift from the Rev. Francis Goodwin, third rector and a member of a prominent and wealthy family, the original church was replaced by the present edifice.

Not surprisingly, this congregation's history and money story as a free church have shaped its ministry over the decades with a strong commitment to and involvement with community outreach. At one point the parish leadership even decided to spend down the endowment for missional initiatives rather than adhere to a more prudent spending policy. Fortunately, the attitude toward endowment spending changed and the vestry is now making efforts to replenish much of the depleted funds. Trinity's founding as a free church is reflected in its commitment to inclusion and diversity in all forms. It also has a tradition of strong lay leadership who actively facilitate and manage the annual stewardship campaign and boldly preach and teach about money, generosity, and the need to support one's faith community. Despite future financial challenges, the congregation is clear about its money legacy as it plans to be a place of welcome, hope, and healing for years to come.

Since we spend significant time in New York City, Margaret and I are also members of a church in the city.

The church was designated a landmark by the New York City Landmark Preservation Commission in 1967, a move opposed at the time by the rector and vestry. Beginning in 1981, the parish became involved in a much-publicized case involving air rights in the highly competitive New York real estate market, which clashed with passionate proponents of historic preservation. The parish's plan to replace the community house with an open terrace and a high-rise commercial structure was opposed by the city, and the U.S. Supreme Court eventually resolved the matter in the city's favor. The controversy resulted in the establishment of a foundation and, later, a wholly independent conservancy. The parish has engaged in significant restoration of the buildings over the last several years.

Despite its reputation and its buildings, the church has a modest endowment as compared with other Manhattan churches and, in addition to membership support, has relied significantly on rental income. Under the leadership of the current rector, stewardship efforts have been significantly enhanced and the proceeds from the sale of air rights have generated funds for building restoration and repair.

Clearly, unlike the other parishes I have been involved with, this congregation's history and money story are complex and involve internal and external conflict that still has repercussions to this day. While the parish may not need or desire to tell its money story in any focused or deliberate way, continued financial transparency is essential to the vitality and sustainability of this important faith community.

While unique and contextual, each of the five parishes discussed in this chapter has a money story that is directly tied to its history and has shaped its mission, vision, ministry, and culture. Furthermore, the money legacies of these faith communities impact their current viability as well as their financial sustainability for the future. My account suggests that not all money legacies or stories are perfect or unblemished. As with all institutions, they include fragile personalities, human foibles, unwise decisions, and even some financial mismanagement. But these stories are also bold accounts of faithful Christians with vision, foresight, and even courage to found and sustain parishes that have made a difference in the lives of their members and their communities for generations.

I encourage these parishes to continue to tell their money stories, because they continue to be relevant, meaningful, and important. As membership and attendance in these and other parishes continue to decline, church money stories and parish financial legacies become more critical to financial sustainability, and even predictors of the future of the larger Episcopal Church.

We will now turn to how and why you should begin a process of telling the money legacies and ongoing money stories of your congregations and its members.

3 ▪ *Telling Your Money Stories*

As I reflect on my personal money story in chapter 1, I realize that it says a lot more about me than just my economic circumstances over the past sixty-five years. It is a story that reflects my family history, especially that of my maternal grandmother, my faith journey, my career ambitions, and my values. It also discusses my partnership with Margaret and how we raised our two sons to honorable adulthood. My money story touches almost every aspect of my life in significant detail and has convinced me how much we can learn about ourselves and one another through the single lens of money.

Now that I have told my personal money story, I encourage you to do the same, maybe not with the same level of detail, but with a sense of purpose, passion, and honesty. By sharing your money story with other members of your congregation, you will be embarking on the beginning of an important journey—a journey that will build up a sense of community and fellowship and enhance your congregation's role as the body of Christ in your unique context. The process of sharing your money stories could be an important tool in raising up new leaders, making disciples for Jesus, and focusing your efforts on gratitude and stewardship. Fortified and inspired by each other's stories, you will be better equipped to be stewards all of God's creation and address the spiritual and human needs of each other and that of a broken world. So how do you begin?

I do not advise that at announcement time one Sunday the priest or lay leader direct that everyone will be required to share their money stories at subsequent parish gatherings. You might get some pushback. While talking about money is a critical and necessary obligation for all faith communities, it is also a sensitive subject. As I indicated earlier, most people are much more comfortable talking about their politics, their medical conditions, or even details about their intimate relationships rather than their money. There are also generational, racial, ethnic, and even geographic differences that need to be understood and appreciated before you embark on this journey. Even the most extroverted and open person may feel that their money story is none of the church's business and nobody needs to know it anyway.

While the Tools and Resources section of this book contains more specific ways of engaging this process, I do want to put them in context and make some general observations and comments. I suggest that you begin this process at the leadership level with the vestry, bishop's committee, or other governing body of the congregation. Ideally, members of these governing bodies are already used to sharing personal information in the context of retreats, Bible studies, or fellowship and social opportunities. But even among these smaller and presumably more connected groups of church members there will be some challenges. The biggest obstacle is that many people will ask why—why do you want to know my money story—the classic "what's it to you" response.

One of the biggest shortcomings of our congregations is that we spend much more time on the "what" or "how" rather than the "why." Before we focus on what we want to do or how we intend to do it, especially with diminishing human and financial resources, we need to go back to basics—Who are we? Why do we exist? And then, what is God calling us to do and how do we get there? This fundamental approach to mission and ministry always needs to be front and center. While there may be designated time for more formal processes around visioning, planning, and strategic direction, asking "why" questions is a dynamic, iterative, and ongoing process. It is interesting that young children ask "why" questions more than any other inquiries, especially when given directions or tasks by adults with authority in their lives. Why is it that we no longer find such questions necessary or appropriate as we grow older and presumably wiser?

While the leadership of a congregation always needs to be able to respond to questions around "why," it is especially critical when dealing with issues around money. One common error in our annual pledge campaigns is that we try to respond to the question of "why give" at the same time we are asking our members to discern when and how much. If stewardship is a way of life for any Christian community, we need to talk about it all year long and not only during the last few months of the year. The pledge drive should be the culmination of a thoughtful, prayerful, spiritually grounded twelve-month process—the icing on the cake, if you will. Similarly, if we believe that our money stories are directly tied to our unique identity, our spiritual journey, and our personal response to all-generous God, making that happen takes a lot of preparation.

The process of sharing our money stories also needs to be gradual, contextual, organic, and nonthreatening. For example, I recall participating in a day-long choir retreat many years ago. It was designed to hone some musical skills outside of the pressure of weekly rehearsal, to build community among members of the choir, and to help us appreciate the strong connection between music and worship. One of the facilitators was the associate rector, who was energetic, personable, and well-liked by the choir, even though he couldn't sing a note. After an opening prayer, he indicated that he was going to ask each of us three questions. The first one was straightforward—"When you were seven years old, how was your family home heated?" Most of the responses indicated oil or natural gas, although I did share a memory of going to the cellar with my father when I was five to watch him stoke the furnace with coke. The second question was almost as innocuous: "Where was the warmest place in your house?" Most people said the kitchen, but one soprano indicated that the warmest place in house focused on the presence of her mother. And then the third question: "When and how did you realize that God loved you?" In response to this question, a significant discussion ensued when people shared their intimate stories about experiencing the love of God, from personal tragedies and triumphs to meaningful celebrations and other remembrances. Clearly, the intent of the exercise was to get to the third question, but the level and tone of the conversation would have been much more strained, if not superficial, without the first two icebreakers.

Perhaps we need a similar approach to the money question. Rather than initially asking members to indicate how their personal experience of money has shaped their lives, you may need to begin with some icebreakers. There are multiple online tools and other resources that one can use to determine a person's money personality. Some are clearly marketing opportunities by investment firms, but most of them are rather informal and fun. Each tool attempts to determine several different money personality types, for example, (a) investors, savers, big spenders, debtors, and shoppers; (b) money worship, avoidance, vigilance, and status, or (c) the more playful categories of amasser, hoarder, avoider, money monk, or spender. My favorite category is "money monk." While you would think that this label represents a spiritually grounded attitude toward money, if you are a money monk, you think that money is dirty, that it is bad, and that if you have too much of it, it will corrupt you. In general, you believe that "money is the root of all evil."

After the group has fun discussing their money personalities, the next logical step may be to begin telling money stories with some level of detail. Once the leadership becomes comfortable with this process, it can then begin to share it with the wider congregation. Once again, you may want to start with something nonthreatening, such as including a link to a money personality quiz in the weekly bulletin or monthly newsletter as a "soft" precursor to the annual pledge campaign. Priests may consider incorporating their personal money story in a sermon, reflection, or blog post. This could be an important modeling exercise for the wider congregation. It is a tangible way of encouraging them or even giving them permission to do the same.

There may also be opportunities for people to tell their money stories during parish forums or town hall meetings when the primary topics are finance and budgets. This can be one way of helping members of the congregation connect with and even take ownership of the financial condition of the parish. I strongly suggest, however, that individual sharing takes place in small groups or even pairs rather than in plenary sessions. This should not be a process that creates unnecessary anxiety, embarrassment, or intimidation. To the contrary, money stories should be opportunities for community building, fellowship, and even fun.

Above all, any process for sharing money stories must be contextual and relevant to the unique circumstances of your congregation, especially your demographics. How, when, and even whether you engage in this process will be influenced by the age, race, ethnicity, gender, and economic status of your members. It will even be affected by your geographic location. This is one situation in which greater diversity may make the process more challenging. People tend to be much more comfortable talking about money within their demographic circles. There are also significant cultural differences around money conversations that need to be appreciated and respected. I strongly suggest that any group planning these kinds of events reflects the various constituencies of the congregation.

Even with these challenges and resulting modifications, any process of encouraging people to share their money stories is still important and worthwhile. I will provide greater details on why this is so in the next chapter. How you do it, however, needs to reflect the unique circumstances of the congregation.

The money legacies and the ongoing money stories of the congregations I have attended over the past forty years, at least from my own perspective, say a lot about how members were engaged in local mission and ministry, especially in the areas of stewardship, generosity, and giving. The financial legacies of these five congregations permeates everything they do and shapes their approach in discerning their role in the community and the wider church. Furthermore, the stories of these parishes have helped to form me as a church leader and have influenced my own spiritual journey. As we continue to experience numerical decline at all levels of the Episcopal Church and navigate through a postpandemic world, we need to develop and implement new and innovative ways of gathering the faithful, forming disciples, and engaging in local mission. This monumental task will require a massive redeployment of human and financial resources and a significant change in our governance and administrative structures. This can only happen effectively if our leaders are willing to examine and analyze every aspect of how we do business as the church, especially around fiscal and budgetary matters. Knowing and telling our institutional money stories will be a key element of this process.

Telling the money story of a congregation should be an easier process since it involves an institution rather than individual members. Nevertheless, the financial situation of any parish has been shaped by individual members over time and managed by specific individuals in key leadership positions, especially the rector. There may even be some sensitivities or lingering hard feelings long after the players are no longer present. The process of discussing the financial legacy of a congregation is not meant to address or handle current situations of financial misconduct or mismanagement. Such serious matters require the immediate intervention of diocesan officials, including outside expertise. But even in the most financially stable congregations, there are cycles of ups and downs that continue to impact current budgetary realities and even the giving patterns of longtime members. When initiating a capital campaign, for example, it is helpful to know the historical details of any prior campaigns and whether they were deemed successful at the time they were initiated. Furthermore, as evidenced in my own congregations, the money stories of any faith community provide context, if not explanation, to current and future annual giving efforts as well as the overall approach to stewardship in general.

While the Tools and Resources provide specific ideas, when telling the money story of a congregation, you should probably start at the beginning, that is, why, when, and how was the congregation founded and funded. In older, established parishes this often involves the history of the wider community as well as its first families and the social and economic movers and shakers. In newer parishes, the founders are often current members and sharing their story is an opportunity to honor them and thank them for their ongoing generosity. In every situation, however, the congregation's money legacy is relevant and even critical to its current and future financial sustainability.

In addition to "founders' days" or patronal feasts, it is also helpful to talk about financial legacy during the annual stewardship campaign and the annual meeting when the budget is presented. Money legacies should be directly tied to financial transparency and used to enforce confidence in current management and operations, especially if they have been improved or enhanced over time. Money histories need to be included in the profile of any parish involved in a search for new clergy leadership. Any priest worth their salt will need this information in discerning a call and a possible match. Finally, telling and sharing a parish's money history is yet another way of engaging the community and creating additional opportunities for fellowship and fun.

Whether we're talking about money on an individual or organizational basis, there are a few simple ground rules we should keep in mind. Brendan O'Sullivan-Hale, the canon to the ordinary in the Diocese of Indianapolis, suggests four lessons he learned regarding talking about money in the church.

He shared these in an ECF *Vestry Papers* article in March 2018 and in ECF's *Finance Resource Guide*:

Lesson 1: Say what you mean. In other words, when you're talking about money, talk about money. Try not to use "stewardship as an obfuscatory euphemism."

Lesson 2: Focus. While Christian stewardship encompasses the three-fold gifts of time, talent, and treasure, talk about treasure, and not the other two, if money is the focus of the conversation.

Lesson 3: Acknowledge the hard stuff. Be aware that money touches us in the deepest places of our lives and may be a source of anxiety and shame.

Lesson 4: Trust God's promise. Always remember that God ultimately rewards our faithfulness.

In addition to these helpful lessons, we must also remember that money is a means and not an end to itself. When Jesus talked about money, even in the most stark terms, he was acknowledging the challenges and difficulties of managing our relationship with money while encouraging us to change and transform. As with everything else he taught, Jesus did this all with incredible love, compassion, and grace.

4 ▪ *Why Money Stories Matter*

Let's elaborate on why the process of telling money legacies and ongoing money stories is so important to local faith communities and their members.

Telling Money Stories by Individuals

Pastoral

As Americans in a consumer society, money tends to sit at the heart of who we are and what we value. The amount of money we have often defines us, as it determines our social and economic status. For people who live paycheck to paycheck, cash flow determines the ability to pay rent and feed families. Because of its importance in who we are and what we do, money is a pastoral issue for local faith communities and their leadership.

In telling our money stories to our congregation, we are revealing an important part of our identity. No matter how much detail we may or may not share, our story provides important information that may suggest a need for current or future pastoral support. For example, a story about economic insecurity or impending job loss may imply a desire for direct financial assistance or a referral to an appropriate governmental agency.

References to excessive debt or living beyond one's means may be a plea for some type of consumer credit counseling. Even stories of economic success or privilege may warrant unique and appropriate individual pastoral responses.

Some pastors may find these suggestions to be inappropriate, intrusive, or beyond the scope of their responsibilities, especially if gleaned through an individual's personal reflections. But why should economic-related issues be any different than those dealing with health, relationships, or grief? Our faithful people come to us from all walks of life and from every human condition. We are called to welcome and embrace them wherever they are on their life journey and, more importantly, to respond to their spiritual and temporal needs, including those relating to money. Spiritual health is directly tied to our relationship to money and the choices we make in its use.

Beyond individual financial concerns, the collective money stories of members of the congregation may indicate a more systemic issue or the need for some parish-wide programs or offerings in areas such as debt reduction, financing college, estate planning, or even bankruptcy protection. Any savvy pastor or priest must be attuned to the individual and collective needs and concerns of the congregation to develop and implement appropriate ministries, programs, and pastoral responses for all members.

Fellowship

One of the primary reasons people join a church is for the sense of belonging to a community. Fellowship and hospitality are key components of community-building in any congregation. Despite the availability of robust online worship during the pandemic, one of the things we all missed the most was the ability to physically interact with other members of the congregation, whether at coffee hour, exchanging the peace, or at the communion rail. Furthermore, we all want and need information about each other as we build relationships within the parish community—where we live, what we do, whether we have spouses, children, grandchildren. In telling our money stories, even at the most basic level, we are sharing information with fellow parishioners and, through that process, are enhancing our relationships on an individual level and helping to build up community throughout the wider parish.

Furthermore, some of the ways of telling our stories as suggested in the Tools and Resources provide new and different opportunities for gathering, sharing, and having fun. Rather than being a source of embarrassment and shame, the process of telling our stories could also result in new friendships, enhanced fellowship, and even joy.

Stewardship

Stewardship is more than just fundraising. It is the life-giving way we respond to God's call in the church and in the world. Nevertheless, as suggested throughout this book, one of the primary ways we demonstrate our commitment as faithful stewards of all of God's creation is through our financial contributions, especially those to or through local faith communities. Our money stories encompass not only our values and priorities, they also reflect and influence our faith journeys as we strive to enhance and perfect our commitment to Christian stewardship in all of its manifestations.

I am perplexed by those priests and pastors who deliberately refuse to know the pledging patterns of individual members of their congregations. The primary reason for this practice, apparently, is not wanting to discriminate or show preference to a congregant based on their giving. This argument suggests a vocational crisis beyond knowing a person's pledge but, more importantly, totally misses the point. The rector or priest needs to know the amount of each person's pledge because it is their spiritual, fiduciary, and pastoral obligation to do so. If stewardship goes to the heart of who we are as Christians, our pastors need to know how much we give because our pledge demonstrates our individual commitment toward this effort.

By knowing our money story, both individually and collectively, the priest can better exercise all three responsibilities. For example, if an individual member, or the congregation as a whole, is not pledging or is underpledging based on information and belief, the priest may need to do a better job of preaching and teaching the spiritual basis of stewardship and giving. Furthermore, the priest, in partnership with the lay leaders, has a fiduciary responsibility to maintain the financial integrity of the parish and pledged income is a key component of a parish budget. Finally, a person's giving or lack thereof is also a pastoral issue. If a member's pledge suddenly or precipitously declines, it might indicate significant dissatisfaction or negative change in economic circumstances. Both are pastoral issues that need to be addressed.

Familiarity with the money stories of the congregation help the parish leadership engage in a process of responsible budgeting and designing an annual pledge campaign that is contextual and reflective of the economic circumstances and money attitudes of the congregation. If the money story process suggests a predominance of fixed incomes or economic distress, the parish leadership will be better prepared to provide an appropriate budgetary response. On the other hand, collective money stories suggesting more economic security than originally anticipated may result in a more ambitious pledge drive goal. At any rate, the process of encouraging and facilitating members of the congregation in telling their money stories can directly enhance the stewardship efforts of the parish, especially the annual pledge campaign.

Leadership

A person's earliest experiences with money in their family of origin can affect and influence their attitude and relationship with money for the rest of their lives. Growing up with economic insecurity or sense of want tends to remain with you even if your financial circumstances significantly improve.

Similarly, growing up with significant financial privilege often clouds a perception of money even if financial conditions deteriorate over time. Obviously, there are no hard and fast rules here. But much like Myers-Briggs or Enneagram personality classifications, money legacies can often explain or even predict a person's ongoing financial attitudes, if not actual behavior. A simple illustration of this premise is the financial habits of those who grew up during the Depression, the so-called "Greatest Generation."

The Greatest Generation is generally defined as people born from 1901 to 1927. They were shaped by the Great Depression and were the primary participants in World War II. Following the war, this generation birthed the Baby Boomers and later became the grandparents of Generation X and Millennials. They came of age during the Roaring Twenties, a time of economic prosperity with distinctive cultural transformations. After the stock market crashed in 1929, this generation experienced profound economic and social turmoil. Some of the characteristics of this generation include personal responsibility, humility, work ethic, commitment, integrity, self-sacrifice, and, above all, frugality. Saving every penny and every scrap helped families survive during times of shortage. "Use it up, wear it out, make it do, or do without" was a motto of their time.

The identification of this demographic cohort around the issue of frugality results from collective money stories of its individual members. My father, a veteran of WWII, was a classic member of the Greatest Generation. He grew up as one of nine children and I am convinced that his fondness for leftovers stemmed from his childhood experience of having an adequate but limited quantity of food at the dinner table.

If a person's money legacy impacts their current attitude and relationship with money, their money story is key to this nexus. Consequently, using money stories as a way of assessing or evaluating a person's capacity for church leadership is probably one of the most interesting and controversial aspects of this premise. While we should never discriminate against or exclude a person from parish leadership based on their financial legacy, how that legacy is reflected in their personal money story can be informative. Much like assessing passions or gifts for ministry, a person's relationship with money may be a relevant factor in discerning their leadership potential.

For example, if your congregation is in the process of recruiting a treasurer or chair of a finance committee, you may not want to select someone who has articulated an unhealthy relationship with money or who has incurred significant and unsustainable debt. Similarly, the coordinator of the annual fundraising campaign should be someone who embraces both the theology and practice of Christian stewardship rather than one with no history of pledging or other expressions of generosity. Rather than a reason for exclusion, however, a person's relationship with money, as gleaned from their story, is just one factor in a more holistic process of recruiting new leaders.

Similarly, a person's money legacy may also help explain their decision-making and thought processes when already in positions of leadership or authority. A vestry member whose family of origin lost a home to creditors may be reluctant to support a decision to take on a building loan for a parish addition. On the other hand, a person with a history of significant financial means may be more readily willing to support parish budgets that are not supported with adequate revenue.

In addition to church leadership, a person's money legacy may also influence their actions and attitudes in their workplace or other nonprofit or community activities. The operative word here is "may." While not determinative or foolproof, a person's money legacy, as revealed in their money story, may be a useful tool in explaining their leadership behavior as well as assessing their suitability to begin with.

Discipleship

While the church is involved in many different ministries and needs to be actively engaging in God's mission in the world, one of its primary roles and responsibilities is to make disciples for Jesus. Discipleship does not happen automatically. It is the result of a deliberate process of formation that involves learning the teachings of Jesus, developing a relationship with him, embracing practices that deepen that relationship, and then living a godly and righteous life in the world. To become a disciple, Christians need to reorder and make right those aspects of their lives that interfere with or inhibit this process. Disciples strive to be in right relationship with God in all aspects of their lives, including money. Developing a right relationship with

God around money is not easy and may even be a lifelong process. Yet cultivating healthy and life-giving attitudes and practices about money, generosity, and stewardship is an essential element of a person's journey toward discipleship.

Confronting our money stories is one tangible way of developing a right relationship with God around this critical aspect of our daily lives. Telling our money stories, much like sharing our faith journeys, helps us understand our past and, more importantly, discern new and healthy attitudes around our economic realities. As disciple-makers, therefore, the church needs to be actively engaged in any process that deepens and enhances our relationship with Jesus. Given the importance of money in our individual and collective lives and its role in distorting our ability to discern God's call, the church is obligated to be directly involved in these critical conversations.

Telling Money Stories
by Congregations

While congregations and local faith communities need to facilitate money conversations among and between their members, they also need to tell their own money stories and confront their own financial legacies. While most church leaders, including clergy, understand why money is important in the life of the community, the harder question is why they need to talk about it. There are several compelling reasons for engaging in the process, and paying the bills is just one of them.

History

The history of Christianity in the world is basically a complex story about money and economic power. The early followers of Jesus (as told in the Acts of the Apostles) shared all their earthly belongings, lived in intentional community, and addressed the needs of widows and orphans. Barnabas was warmly welcomed when he donated all his wealth to the original apostles. While this closed economy worked well for a while, the exponential growth of the church required, or at least enjoyed, expanded financial resources and eventually the power, prestige, and riches of the Roman Empire. From the time of Constantine through Gregory the Great, Charlemagne, the Medici popes, Henry VIII, and even up to the present, the story of the Christian church is directly linked to economic and political power and marred by violence, corruption, and exploitation.

Likewise, the history of the Episcopal Church in the United States is also tied to our country's financial and economic growth and development. Beginning as a fledgling cult identified with the defeated Loyalists after the American Revolution in the late 1700s, the Episcopal Church gained significant wealth and prestige over the next century, becoming the quasi-established church and boasting eleven US presidents, dozens of senators, and multiple industrialists and financiers of the Gilded Age. Many of our most historic and cherished Episcopal parishes and institutions were founded by people of immense wealth who built elegant temples as memorials to their legacy and often included endowments for their maintenance and support in perpetuity. The history of these places is directly and profoundly linked to money.

Even in more modest circumstances and in "newer" states and geographic areas, the history of parishes and church buildings is directly tied to the money legacy of the congregation. There is no church institution that has not required an initial capital investment, especially for the bricks and mortar we have all come to know and love. While the more recent schism in the Episcopal Church started as a theological conflict over biblical interpretation and human sexuality, it soon became a legal battle for money and property. Several congregations in the continuing Diocese of Fort Worth lost their properties to the Anglican Church in North America through a court battle, and this historical anomaly will profoundly impact their future viability and sustainability. Congregations need to tell their money stories and share their money legacies because these conversations reflect their history, their resilience, and their very purpose for being.

Transparency

Congregations have a legal, moral, and practical obligation for transparency in all their financial and business dealings. Such transparency requires committed lay and clergy leadership, open communication, and internal controls manifested through regular reporting and annual audits. Churches that are transparent in their operations and financial matters trend to do better than those that are not. Furthermore, transparency often leads to growth and healthy stewardship because it encourages members and especially newcomers to join, contribute, and participate in the life of the congregation.

While financial transparency is usually focused on current and future operations, a congregation needs to be open and honest about its past financial history, especially if there have been periods of financial indifference, mismanagement, or even fraud. Telling the money story of the congregation, both positive and negative, in conjunction with ongoing sound financial practices and internal controls demonstrates to the membership and the wider community that your parish has learned from any mistakes of the past and now stewards its financial resource wisely, appropriately, and missionally.

Stewardship and Fundraising

Much like transparency, telling the money story of the congregation is yet another way of assuring donors that the parish has understood and appreciated the need for sound financial management from the very beginning. Even in those situations without a clean financial history, telling the story is a way for the leadership to acknowledge past faults and transgressions and explain how these deficiencies have been addressed and rectified.

While telling the financial story of a congregation should be a regular part of the annual stewardship campaign, it is especially critical when launching a capital campaign or a special appeal. Current donors want and need to know how money for major projects has been raised in the past and why it may be time for another appeal or campaign. If a prior campaign has been unsuccessful for whatever reason, the leadership needs to acknowledge it, admit it, and explain why this campaign will be different.

Telling money stories is also important in initiating and sustaining a planned giving program or establishing a legacy society. Most parish endowments came into being though the generosity and faithfulness of members from years past. Many of these gifts, usually through estates, were fairly modest at the time, but through capital appreciation and additional gifts grew into the endowment corpus that is helping to fund current and future ministries. Planned giving donors need to know that like the "communion of saints" they are a part of a past, present, and future band of witnesses supporting their beloved faith community.

Transitions

Parishes are required to disclose their current financial status to diocesan officials prior to initiating a search. This information is used to determine their capacity for funding a rector or priest and at what level. The current reality is that for many congregations, upon the retirement or resignation of their rector they are no longer able to financially support a full-time successor. Thus, current financial information provides important and practical data in the congregation's readiness for the process.

I would also suggest that the money legacy of the congregation is also relevant to the search process for new clergy leadership. First, it proclaims a level of financial transparency that tells would-be candidates that the congregation has nothing to hide. Additionally, the money legacy of the parish provides key insights into current and prospective financial health. For example, the money story may explain why a congregation is overly reliant on endowment income and has never embraced an effective approach to stewardship. Furthermore, the money history may indicate how the parish has handled past periods of economic challenges and provide key insights into current and future strategies and approaches. Finally, if the congregation wants to attract the most appropriate priest possible, it needs to provide all the information necessary for that priest to discern and respond to a call.

Times of transition are key opportunities for transformation and change. A congregation's confronting and acknowledging its financial past during a search process may help shape its ministry for years to come.

Sustainability

Finally, we are approaching a time when many of our congregations will need to close, merge, or re-form because they are no longer economically sustainable. Obviously this is a complex and delicate issue and requires prayerful, thoughtful, and strategic process. It also requires information and data and significant opportunities for members of the congregation to evaluate, celebrate, and mourn. Since these decisions are often based on money rather than missional viability, knowing the money legacy becomes critical in evaluating the current financial picture. Additionally, it is a tangible way for the members of the congregation, especially the leadership, to connect with the past at the same time they are discerning their future.

5 ▪ *Putting It All Together and Next Steps*

Over the past several chapters we have explored the process of telling individual and congregational money stories and why it is important, especially in these times. While the Episcopal Church is extremely diverse in terms of size, budget, geography, demographics, and contexts in which its parishes and missions operate, we are primarily a denomination of small congregations. In 2019, the median average Sunday worship attendance was only fifty-one. Only 4 percent of congregations had an average Sunday attendance (ASA) of three hundred or more, and 75 percent have an ASA of one hundred or fewer. Smaller congregations have significant advantages, including greater financial transparency, easier communications, invested members, opportunities for innovation, and a sense that we are all in this together. On the other hand, smaller congregations rely on volunteers and leaders since they have smaller budgets and income streams. The leadership often feels burned out and everyone tends to experience frustration and disappointment when things go wrong. Because everyone knows one another, members of smaller congregations may also have privacy concerns, especially when it comes to money. Even in presumably anonymous situations, people can often figure out who is doing what, saying what, or giving what.

Larger congregations also may have issues in creating and sustaining a money story process. Leaders may think that this should be a staff-driven process, and while they may support it in principle initially, may decide not to actively participate. Because of the diversity of opinions and the greater probability of strong opinion leaders in larger congregations, there may be a greater number of people who believe and articulate that telling money stories is not the business of the church.

I am also aware that the level of comfort around money talk is often related to race, ethnicity, age, and economic status. The elders of some ethnic groups are often reluctant to talk about money in front of children and even the idea of articulating a pledge amount in advance is somewhat of an anathema. Much like the system of supporting churches through pew rentals in the nineteenth and early part of the twentieth centuries, the idea of an annual pledge is a white, Anglo, upper-middle-class phenomenon that is not universally embraced. In some circles, even the term "stewardship" or "steward" connotes overseers on Caribbean plantations rather than faithful and generous Christians. For this reason, it may be preferable to use words like "generosity," "participation," and "celebration" to describe the process of supporting a local faith community.

Given these realities, however, I want to suggest the following next steps for any congregation to determine whether, why, and how it would like to pursue a money legacy process, and given the polity and structure of the Episcopal Church I would start this conversation at the vestry level.

Begin with Prayer and Bible Study

Like everything we do as a church, we begin by inviting God into the process and allowing the Holy Spirit to do her work. Bible study is a good spiritual discipline but also an opportunity for people to share their thoughts and feelings in a nonthreatening way. The African Bible study process, for example, initially asks participants to share a word or phrase that jumps out at them during the reading and hearing of a passage and eventually to discern what the scripture is calling the group to do in that particular time and place.

Lectio Divina can also be an effective tool because it requires participants to put themselves right in the middle of the passage. For example, how would you feel as the rich young man who is told by Jesus to shed all of his belongings in order to achieve salvation? In addition to the passages quoted in the Introduction, the Tools and Resources contain other suggestions for an appropriate and contextual Bible study.

Ask the Question "Why?"

While I have provided reasons for engaging in the process of sharing money legacies and ongoing money stories, each congregation needs to come to its own conclusion. Timing may be an issue, as evidenced by the limitations of the recent pandemic. On the other hand, emerging from the COVID-19 pandemic may also be an opportune time to begin this process.

While some time periods may be more convenient than others, it is always appropriate and timely to talk about money in the church context because finances permeate and encompass every aspect of local mission and ministry.

Recognize That Talking about Money Can Be Difficult

As part of asking the "why" question, gauge the comfort level of people in the room in moving forward with the process. I assume that there may be widely different opinions, especially in larger and more diverse congregations. Ask vestry members to describe the scope and level of the comfort. Make sure people feel safe about expressing their opinions and feelings. Be comfortable with moments of silence and periods of ambivalence. Whatever decision is made, however, it should be done by consensus. A divided vote means that the leadership is not yet ready for this process. Any decision can always be revisited at a more opportune time.

Start Slow but Be Clear about Your Intent

As indicated by Canon Brendan O'Sullivan-Hale in 2018: "When you're talking about money, talk about money." The conversation at this level should not be about stewardship, budgeting, or pledging—it's about money, pure and simple. While it may be appropriate to start the vestry conversation with something less threatening like a money personality quiz, at some point the conversation needs to be much more focused and direct. In order for this process to be effective and life-giving, ultimately each participant needs to tell their money story from their family of origin to the present, focusing on their attitudes and relationships with money with as much detail as possible. There will be plenty of other opportunities to resort to more global issues of income, expenses, and stewardship campaigns.

Start at the Top

Managing the financial resources of a congregation of any size is a collaborative process that requires effective lay-clergy partnerships. When talking about money or sharing money legacies, however, the rector or priest may need to go first. First, many clergy have significant issues around money conversations even though financial management is a key component of their responsibilities and duties. Many also lack the capacity to manage their own personal finances as well. The Lilly Endowment established the National Initiative to Address Economic Challenges Facing Pastoral Leaders based on research that indicated the need for clergy to develop financial literacy in both the personal and organizational contexts. The Episcopal Church Foundation (ECF) participated in this initiative and has developed ongoing programs that deal with these issues.

Clergy need to confront their own fears and discomfort around money talk in order to encourage their lay leaders and members to the same. Furthermore, having the priest go first is a good modeling exercise and may even encourage reluctant leaders or members to participate in this process. Once the clergy tell their story, it may be followed by a warden, treasurer, or other senior lay leader. This is a great opportunity for individual lay leaders to step up to the plate.

Make Sure That Both the Individual and Congregational Storytelling Processes Are Coordinated and Aligned

While both processes do not need to start at the same time, it is helpful for members of the congregation to understand how they are coordinated and aligned. The congregation's money legacy story may be more prominent during the annual pledge drive or the budget rollout, for example, with individual stories occurring during other times in the year. Both conversations are critical to the financial health and well-being of the faith community and need to be comprehensive, seamless, and as simultaneous as possible.

The Process Must Be Presented as a Spiritual Practice Rather Than a Fundraising Exercise

Once a decision is made to go forward, it must be explained as a spiritual practice and not be viewed as a ruse to get people to increase their pledge or contribute to a special appeal. The ultimate byproduct may be increased giving or an enhanced sense of stewardship. The point of the process, however, is for people to confront and share their own money stories and that of their faith community with the goal of developing healthier and more life-giving money attitudes and relationships. Accordingly, this process must be rolled out through spiritually grounded sermons, newsletter articles, or even all-parish virtual or in-person gatherings.

Expect Pushback and Setbacks

This may not be a linear process. Leaders who embrace it initially may pull back as the conversations become more uncomfortable or intense. Storytelling sessions may deteriorate into emotional outbursts and even generate conflict and dissent. Make sure that those persons who facilitate these processes have enough emotional intelligence to navigate these challenges with patience, tact, and grace. While it is always appropriate to pause or slow down the process, I caution against total abandonment once a decision has been made to go forward. Such a response not only diminishes the role and authority of the vestry, but it can also negatively impact the long-term financial well-being of the congregation.

Do Your Homework

Take the time you need to reach consensus on the vestry, prepare an implementation plan and articulate a spiritually grounded reason for going forward. Make sure that the leaders and facilitators are trained and prepared. Pray, practice, and pray again. Devise and implement a process that is focused, life-giving, and fun.

Consider a Year-Round Approach to Conversations about Money, Generosity, and Stewardship

Earlier I cautioned against money conversations being misconstrued as fundraising ploys. That does not mean that money legacy conversations should not occur within the rhythm of the church year, including those opportunities to talk about generosity and giving. Since stewardship should be a yearlong conversation rather than just a topic for discussion during six weeks in the fall, a coordinated plan for money conversations may be appropriate and helpful. The Tools and Resources include a suggested timeline for such an approach.

Conclusion

In his seminal book *Bowling Alone: The Collapse and Revival of American Community,* published in 2000, Robert D. Putnam demonstrates how social capital increased between 1900 and the late 1960s and then dramatically decreased as a result of generational differences, television, urban sprawl, and increasing pressures of time and money. He defines social capital as the connections among the social networks of individuals, including political, civic, and religious participation, workplace and informal networks, and even mutual trust and altruism. Putnam argues that this phenomenon has resulted in a variety of problems, including social conflict, and that the solution to addressing these problems is developing new and innovative forms of social capital going forward.

While some of Putnam's data and conclusions may be dated, especially given recent events, the religious landscape of the United States continues to change at a rapid pace. According to a Gallup research study released in March 2021, America's membership in houses of worship continued to decline in 2020, dropping below 50 percent for the first time in an eight-decade trend. This decline is primarily a function of the increasing number of Americans who express no religious preference growing from 13 percent in 2008–10 to 21 percent in 2017–20.

Furthermore, church membership is strongly correlated with age, with those in older generations more likely to be church members than their younger counterparts.

Clearly, the Episcopal Church has been a victim of these generational trends. Our membership and average Sunday attendance have consistently declined about 5 percent each year, and statistically, if nothing changes, there will be nobody in the pews by the year 2040. And we are still determining the impact of the pandemic on longer-term membership, attendance, and participation.

Numbers do not tell the full story, though we do need some critical mass of faithful members to carry on the tradition and engage in God's mission in the world from our unique Episcopal perspective. Despite these trends, however, there is some amazing ministry going on, especially at the local level. Congregations managed to provide robust, online worship and formation opportunities and even maintained socially distanced outreach activities to their local communities during the dark days of COVID-19. The Episcopal Church has been a prophetic voice for social justice and racial reconciliation during a period when systemic racism has reared its ugly head once again. The real question is how we affirm such steadfastness, while at the same time acknowledge and recognize that it can no longer be business as usual.

While the Episcopal Church will not die, it will look very different—smaller, leaner, flexible, innovative, and much more missionally focused. And this new model will not occur by happenstance. We need to reform and restructure every aspect of our ecclesial life, from our governance structures to the way we distribute human and financial resources. This will require some controversial steps like conjoining dioceses and closing, merging, or reconfiguring local congregations. These matters are complex and beyond the scope of the present conversation.

Nevertheless, this little book may be a significant step in navigating the Episcopal Church of the future. Since money is central to missional identity and organizational survival, any new model for a future Episcopal Church needs to be financially sustainable. Furthermore, many of the decisions to close, merge, or re-form dioceses, congregations, and other institutions will be based on their current and anticipated financial stability. Therefore, in order for congregations to plan and anticipate their role and place in the Episcopal Church of the future, they need to start talking about money in an open and honest way right now.

The conversations suggested in this book are not only about money, but also about individual and institutional presence, resilience, and faithfulness. They are the combined stories of pilgrims on their journey of faith, trying to find meaning and purpose in their lives through a relationship with others and with Jesus. They are the intimate details of people's hopes, dreams, tragedies, and triumphs. They are tales of personal connections and caring communities. They are about life, love, birth, death, and ultimately transformation.

It all started with stories—of creation and the flood, of deliverance and the law, of covenant and the prophets, of promise and salvation. And these stories have become our stories and continue to this very day. As we tell the money stories of our churches and our members, let us remember that this is a small but important first step in the renewal, rejuvenation, and even rebirth of that part of the body of Christ known as the Episcopal Church.

Tools and Resources

Engaging individuals and congregations in conversations about money can be challenging. Let the tools and resources below inspire you to try a variety of approaches and to be open to the leading of the Holy Spirit.

For Individuals

There are many ways to begin to explore our individual relationships with money:

Conversation Starters for Personal Money Stories
(Answer them for yourself, with a partner, or in small groups.)

- What does money mean to you?

- What did you learn about money in your family of origin?

- In what ways has money impacted your life positively or negatively?

- What does popular culture say about money?

- Why do you think that Jesus has harsh words about money?

- What do you want for yourself in a relationship with money?

- What about money would you like to let go of?

Personal Reflection about Money

Recall and write down a story about a time that money affected your life. Describe what role God played in the story. Consider sharing it in a group.

Exploring Money Personalities

Encouraging a group to explore their "money personalities" together can offer a lighthearted approach to a challenging and sometimes difficult subject.

- ECF Vital Practices Webinar "Money—What's It to You?" (https://www.ecfvp.org/webinars/199/money-whats-it-to-you) explores how our ideas about money are shaped, and how they influence our congregations.

Online quizzes have become popular learning tools. A web search on "money personality quiz" will yield a wide variety of choices. Here are some favorites:

- The Money Harmony Quiz will show you which of five major money personality types most closely matches your own tendencies: Hoarder, Spender, Money Monk, Avoider, or Amasser. https://www.moneyharmony.com/moneyharmony-quiz. The quiz is also available in *Money Harmony: A Road Map for*

Individuals and Couples by Olivia Mellan and Sherry Christie.

- The Klontz Money Script Inventory-II (KMSI-II) helps identify four common attitudes toward money: Money Worship, Money Avoidance, Money Vigilance, and Money Status: http://www.moneyscripts.com/.

- A shorter version is available through NerdWallet, a site devoted to helping individuals get the most from their money: https://www.nerdwallet.com/article /finance/money-personality.

- Sorted, a New Zealand site, offers a lighthearted quiz that reveals financial strengths and possible blind spots: https://sorted.org.nz/tools /money-personality-quiz.

- Dave Ramsey is well known for his Financial Peace University and EveryDollar. While his approach to money management is controversial, you might want to check out his money personality quiz. It examines the natural tendency to be either more of a saver or more of a spender—or as Ramsey calls them, a Nerd or a Free Spirit: https://cdn.ramseysolutions.net /media/pdf/NerdFreeSpiritQuiz.pdf

- Empower offers the Money Psychology Quiz as an opportunity to explore what makes you tick and reveal your relationship with money. Idealist? Stockpiler? Celebrity? https://empower.me/quiz/.

- Myers-Briggs and Marcus by Goldman Sachs have teamed up to help you understand your financial habits. https://www.cnbc.com/select/financial-personality-quiz/.

- *Financial Times* offers a money psychology quiz that helps determine your financial personality—hoarder? Splasher? https://ig.ft.com/sites/quiz/psychology-of-money/. And the link on that page points to a related article explaining each personality's behaviors: https://www.ft.com/content/5e8da24c-bb09-11e6-8b45-b8b81dd5d080.

Books about Money and Faith

- *Being Consumed: Economics of Christian Desire* by William T. Cavanaugh

- *Crucial Conversations: Tools for Talking When Stakes Are High* by Kerry Patterson, Joseph Grenny, Ron McMillan, and Al Switzler

- *Money and Faith: The Search for Enough*, edited and compiled by Michael Schut

- *Sharing Possessions: What Faith Demands* by Luke Timothy Johnson

- *Seven Stages of Money Maturity, The* by George Kinder

- *Woman's Book of Money and Spiritual Vision, The* by Rosemary Williams

For Congregations

Any of the books listed above could be used for a small group study as well as for individual growth. For those who choose to engage their congregation in increasing their understanding of their corporate money legacies, those conversations can begin with ECF's *Finance Resource Guide* (https://www.ecfvp .org/tools/245/finance-resource-guide-tools-and-resources). The *FRG* is designed as a handbook for congregations and vestries, providing in-depth financial management practices and principles and promoting year-round, theologically driven stewardship.

Helping congregations have conversations about money and whole-life stewardship is an essential task for leaders, responding to God's call to "have no other gods before me." Listed below are a number of approaches that can be fruitful in beginning and continuing those conversations.

Conversation Starters about Stewardship

- What would Jesus vote for in your congregation's budget?
- How do people in your congregation learn to be stewards?
- How might you grow your own personal practice of stewardship?
- How does your congregation form believers who are grateful and generous in the way they choose to live their lives?

Books about Stewardship

- *A Spirituality of Fundraising* by Henri J. M. Nouwen
- *Fearless Church Fundraising: The Practical and Spiritual Approach to Stewardship* by Charles LaFond
- *Creating Congregations of Generous People* by Michael Durall

Conversation Starters about Financial Leadership

- How are you inviting new leaders into financial leadership and allowing them to discern how to best use their gifts?
- What story does your congregation's balance sheet tell about your congregation?
- What concrete step can you take in improving how your congregation communicates about finances?
- How does your vestry model your collective theology of money?
- Is your spending aligned with your congregation's mission and vision? What old thing might God be inviting you to lay down in order to do a new thing?
- How might you increase the spiritual support offered to your financial leaders?

Books about Financial Leadership

- *Finance Resource Guide*—Episcopal Church Foundation https://www.episcopalfoundation.org /programs/ecf-publications/frg

- *Humble and Strong: Mutually Accountable Leadership in the Church* by Gerald W. Keucher

Activity Suggestion

Plan a history day for your congregation. As a group, develop a timeline that tells how your congregation began and what has happened over time. Examine the role of money and finances at each stage in that history. See https://www.ecfvp .org/blogs/3739/exploring-your-congregations-financial-history.

Passages for Scripture Study

- 2 Samuel 7:1–7: God's promise to David

- Jeremiah 29:4–7, 11–14: Seek the good of the city

- Mark 8:22–26: The gradual healing of the blind man

- Luke 10:1–12: The sending of the seventy

- Romans 16: Personal greetings and final instructions

- Ephesians 4: Unity in the body of Christ

- Colossians 1:9–23: Christ among the work of the Colossians

Possible Questions to Explore

- What is the difference between God's idea of "enough" and ours? How can we most closely align with God's idea?

- What encourages us to look beyond our perceived limitations? What holds us back?

- Especially when times are tough, how do you know who and what you can count on? What encourages you to have hope?

Year-Round Stewardship

Congregations can make significant progress in becoming wise whole-life stewards when leadership approaches stewardship development as a year-round process. Below is a suggested calendar for a year-long process that can help the congregation adopt a whole-life pattern of stewardship and creatively explore their money legacies. In succeeding years, leadership can continue the practice of preaching and teaching about money and stewardship throughout the year.

July/August

- Summer picnic—fun exercises about money personalities; parish history timeline

- Recruit leadership team for annual stewardship campaign

September

- Begin the program year
- Introduce the concept of money legacies through sermon and adult forum
- Celebrate the ways that, through this year's budget, the congregation has contributed to the life of the community and the faith development of the church

October

- Launch annual fall fundraising campaign for the coming budget year
- Organize "chancel talks" or personal testimonies that include personal money stories and "why I give"
- Promote the ways that next year's budget can help build relationships, serve the community, and contribute to faith formation

November

- Focus on the "saints" of the parish
- Acknowledge Legacy Society members and what legacy funds are accomplishing in the life of the congregation
- In-gathering of pledges
- Thank people who pledge through phonathon and personal notes

December

- Conversations about holiday excess and the true meaning of Christmas
- Highlight the gifts that the congregation shares with one another and the larger community

January

- Conversations about New Year's resolutions, including those about money
- Follow up on lapsed pledgers
- Annual parish meeting—present annual budget in the context of parish money story

February

- Discussion around Lenten disciplines, including those dealing with almsgiving
- Examine the ways that growth in faith encourages growth in our understanding of whole-life stewardship and vice versa

March/April

- Celebrate Lent and Easter
- Focus on "stewardship of nature" with the coming of spring

May

- Pentecost—birth of the church—reprise on money story of congregation
- Recruit new members of Legacy Society

June

- Focus on unpaid or delinquent pledges prior to summer
- Personal conversations about vacations